A Guide to
AMERICAN STATES

Alaska

THE LAST FRONTIER

MEDIA ENHANCED BOOKS
AV2
BY WEIGL
ADDED VALUE · AUDIO VISUAL

www.av2books.com

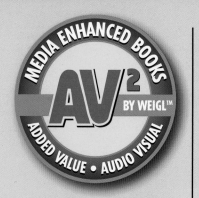

AV² provides enriched content that supplements and complements this book. Weigl's AV² books strive to create inspired learning and engage young minds in a total learning experience.

Your AV² Media Enhanced books come alive with...

Audio
Listen to sections of the book read aloud.

Key Words
Study vocabulary, and complete a matching word activity.

Go to **www.av2books.com**, and enter this book's unique code.

Video
Watch informative video clips.

Quizzes
Test your knowledge.

BOOK CODE

C 1 9 1 3 6 6

Embedded Weblinks
Gain additional information for research.

Slide Show
View images and captions, and prepare a presentation.

AV² by Weigl brings you media enhanced books that support active learning.

Try This!
Complete activities and hands-on experiments.

... and much, much more!

Published by AV² by Weigl
350 5th Avenue, 59th Floor
New York, NY 10118
Website: www.av2books.com   www.weigl.com

Library of Congress Cataloging-in-Publication Data

Strudwick, Leslie, 1970-
  Alaska / Leslie Strudwick.
    p. cm. -- (A guide to American states)
Includes index.
ISBN 978-1-61690-774-7 (hardcover : alk. paper) -- ISBN 978-1-61690-449-4 (online)
1. Alaska--Juvenile literature. I. Title.
F904.3.S793 2011
979.8--dc22
                2011018313

Printed in the United States of America in North Mankato, Minnesota

052011
WEP180511

Project Coordinator Jordan McGill
Art Director Terry Paulhus

Photo Credits
Every reasonable effort has been made to trace ownership and to obtain permission to reprint copyright material. The publishers would be pleased to have any errors or omissions brought to their attention so that they may be corrected in subsequent printings.

Weigl acknowledges Getty Images as its primary image supplier for this title.
Photo of glacier on page 7 courtesy of Edward A. Thomas.
Photos of Leonhard Seppala, Elizabeth Peratrovich, and Benny Benson on pages 32 and 33 courtesy of the Alaska State Library.

Contents

Blanket tossing is an activity in which Alaska Native hunters are tossed into the air for whale-spotting purposes.

Introduction

Alaska is the most northerly state in the United States. Almost one-third of Alaska is within the Arctic Circle. It has a cold climate, rough land, open **tundra**, and few inhabitants. Alaska is sometimes called the Land of the Midnight Sun. During the summer months the sun sets very late in the day. In the northernmost regions the sun does not go below the horizon for almost three months at a time. Imagine, for example, bright sunshine at 2 o'clock in the morning. In the winter, however, daylight is very limited in these areas. Then you might have lunch as you watch the sun setting over the Arctic Ocean.

Mount McKinley in Denali National Park is the tallest mountain in North America.

There are about 900,000 caribou in Alaska, in 32 herds. Most of them live on the treeless tundra.

The name *Alaska* means "mainland" or "great land" in the language of the Aleuts, an Alaska Native group. Alaska is truly a great land. The area of Alaska makes up almost one-fifth of the total area of the United States. Both geography and climate have made it difficult to develop and explore Alaska. It is indeed, as the state's nickname says, the United States' last frontier.

Yet Alaska has played an important part in the history of the nation. Alaska was purchased from Russia in 1867, nearly a century before it became the 49th state in 1959. Miners from the lower 48 U.S. states traveled to Alaska in search of gold in the late 1800s. Many of these settlers fell in love with the wilderness and chose to stay. These new settlers lived among the Alaska Natives, who had inhabited the region for thousands of years.

Where Is Alaska?

Most of Alaska's land forms the largest peninsula in the Western Hemisphere. The state is not connected to the other 48 states of the mainland United States. Instead, most of it juts westward from Canada's Yukon Territory into the Arctic Ocean and the Bering Sea. Southwest of Alaska's mainland stretches the state's long island chain, the Aleutians. Some of the Aleutians lie so far to the west of the mainland that they are within the Eastern Hemisphere.

Extending to the southeast from the Alaska peninsula is a strip of land called the Panhandle. This part of Alaska borders the Canadian province of British Columbia.

Alaska is a remote state, making it difficult for people to travel to or within the state. Travelers reach the state either by way of a couple of highways through Canada or by boat or plane. There are few highways that run through the state.

Seaplanes equipped with **pontoons** are known as floatplanes. Floatplanes are often the way people get into and out of Alaska's remote regions.

The capital city, Juneau, can be reached only by boat or plane. This is also true of many of the state's smaller cities and towns. Nevertheless, the largest city in the state, Anchorage, has all the conveniences of a large city, including planes, trains, roads, museums, universities, and numerous recreational activities.

Alaska's scenic beauty offers wonderful outdoor opportunities for residents and tourists alike. Among the popular pastimes are hiking in the mountains, sailing past **glaciers**, and enjoying the dazzling northern lights. Alaska also attracts adventure seekers who glide over the icy tundra in dogsleds.

Alaska's landscape contains many mountains and includes 17 of North America's 20 tallest peaks. Mount McKinley, at 20,320 feet, is North America's tallest peak, attracting expert mountain climbers to scale its snowfield-covered rock.

Part of the Yukon River forms the border between Alaska and Canada.

Alaska has five different climatic zones. They are Arctic, continental, transitional, and two maritime.

No interstate highways are found in Alaska.

The Alaska Highway was designed during World War II as an emergency measure to provide an overland military supply route to Alaska. It runs more than 1,500 miles through Canada's Yukon Territory to Fairbanks, Alaska.

Mapping Alaska

Alaska is bordered by the Arctic Ocean and the Beaufort Sea to the north. On the east, it shares a border with the Yukon Territory and British Columbia, both part of Canada. To the south, the Gulf of Alaska and the Pacific Ocean form its border. The Bering Strait and the Bering Sea lie to its west. Alaska's Little Diomede Island in the Bering Strait is only 2.5 miles from the border of Russia.

Sites and Symbols

STATE SEAL
Alaska

STATE BIRD
Willow Ptarmigan

STATE FLOWER
Forget-Me-Not

STATE FLAG
Alaska

STATE MAMMAL
Moose

STATE TREE
Sitka Spruce

Nickname The Last Frontier

Motto North to the Future

Song "Alaska's Flag," words by Marie Drake and music by Elinor Dusenbury

Entered the Union Jan. 3, 1959, as the 49th state

Capital Juneau

Population (2010 Census) 710,231 Ranked 47th state

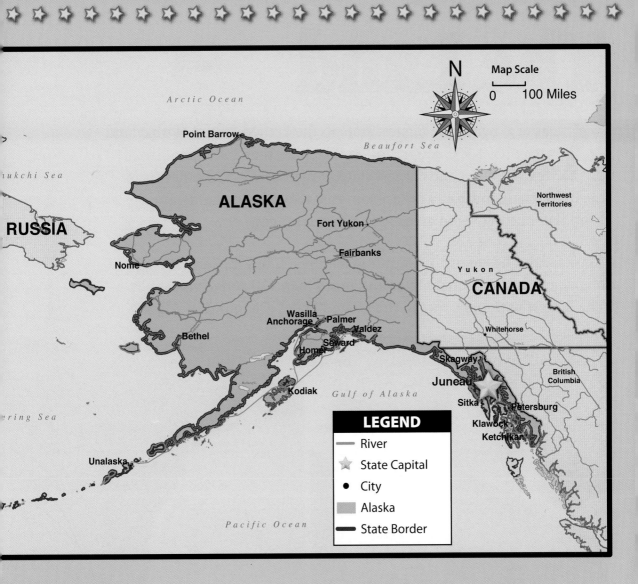

N

Map Scale

0   100 Miles

Arctic Ocean

Point Barrow

ALASKA

hukchi Sea

RUSSIA

Nome

Fort Yukon

Fairbanks

Beaufort Sea

Northwest
Territories

Yukon

CANADA

Whitehorse

Bethel

Wasilla
Anchorage Palmer
Seward Valdez
Homer

Skagway

Juneau

British
Columbia

Sitka

Petersburg

Klawock

Ketchikan

Kodiak

Gulf of Alaska

ering Sea

Unalaska

Pacific Ocean

LEGEND
—	River
⭐	State Capital
•	City
▬	Alaska
▬	State Border

STATE CAPITAL

Juneau has been the capital of Alaska since 1906. Located in southeastern Alaska on the Gastineau Channel, Juneau has a population of about 31,000. It is sheltered from the Pacific Ocean by a belt of islands. In 1970, Juneau merged with the city of Douglas, located on an island across the channel. It is now 3,248 square miles in area, the largest city in area in the United States.

United States

Hawai'i   Alaska

The Land

Alaska is by far the biggest state in the United States. With a land area of 571,951 square miles, it is more than twice the size of Texas, the second-largest state. It measures 1,420 miles from north to south and 2,400 miles from east to west. The land varies from flat, bush-covered areas to mountain ranges.

Alaska's land has many outstanding features. It has the largest number of glaciers in the United States and more than 130 active volcanoes. The largest national parks in the United States are found in Alaska.

WRANGELL–ST. ELIAS NATIONAL PARK

Wrangell–St. Elias National Park is the country's largest national park. It measures more than 20,000 square miles. Nine states are smaller than the park.

ALASKA'S COASTLINE

Alaska's coastline extends for more than 6,600 miles. Including islands, the state has nearly 34,000 miles of shoreline.

DENALI NATIONAL PARK

Permafrost ground underlies many areas of Denali National Park. Only a thin layer of topsoil is available to support life. To survive, plants must be adapted to the cold winters and the short growing season.

TRACY ARM FJORD

Some tidewater glaciers have especially dense ice that causes them to appear blue.

Alaska has around 100,000 glaciers, more active glaciers and ice fields than in any other inhabited place in the world.

The Yukon River, which begins in Canada and is almost 2,000 miles long, flows west across Alaska and empties into the Bering Sea.

About 5,000 earthquakes a year occur in Alaska. Of the 10 strongest earthquakes ever recorded, 3 have occurred in Alaska.

Point Barrow is the northernmost point in the United States. Polar bears are some of the residents of Point Barrow.

An iceberg is a floating mass of freshwater ice that has broken off of either a glacier or an ice shelf. Blue icebergs are more dense than white icebergs.

Climate

The beauty of the Alaskan landscape makes up for the sometimes less-than-pleasant climate. The temperatures in the south are quite mild in summer. The west, which borders the ocean, receives more rain and snow and is often cooler than the rest of the state. In the north, temperatures can hover near the freezing point in July. However, the majority of people living in and visiting Alaska are in the south and central regions of the state. They may experience temperatures of –40° Fahrenheit in the winter, but they enjoy an average summer temperature of about 55°F.

Average Annual Precipitation Across Alaska

There can be huge differences in the amount of precipitation that cities in different parts of Alaska typically receive. What do you think causes these differences?

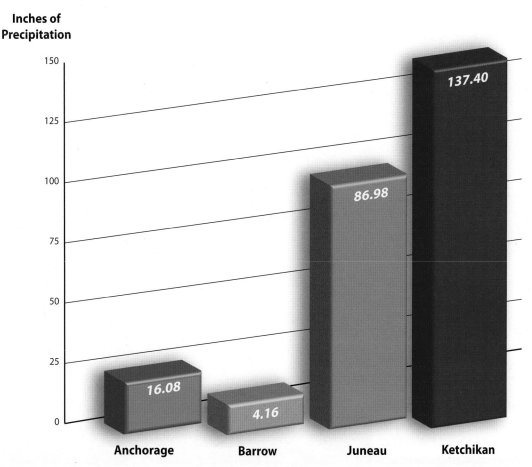

Inches of Precipitation

- Anchorage: 16.08
- Barrow: 4.16
- Juneau: 86.98
- Ketchikan: 137.40

Natural Resources

A laska is rich in natural resources. There are fish in the water, trees covering the land, and minerals in the ground. Gold was the first natural resource that brought prosperity and settlers to Alaska. Large amounts of gold were discovered beginning in the 1870s, drawing thousands of **prospectors** to the area in search of the precious metal. Gold mining still exists today, but it does not employ as many workers as before. There are also mines for coal, silver, and zinc.

Alaska's two main foreign **exports** are precious metals and fish. In fact, the state is the nation's top exporter of fish. Leading catches include salmon, halibut, and shellfish such as crab. Fishing contributes nearly $2 billion to the state's economy each year.

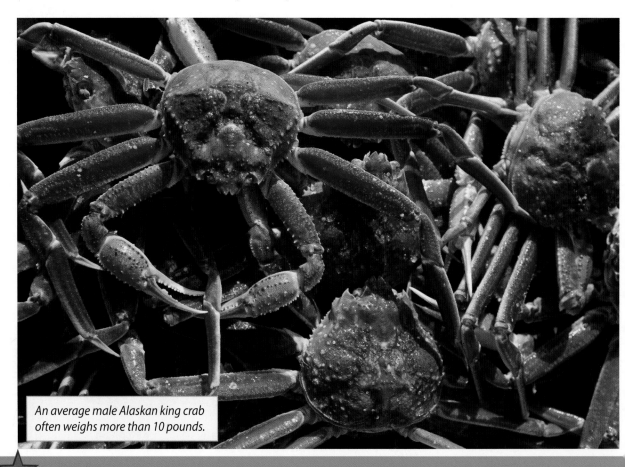

An average male Alaskan king crab often weighs more than 10 pounds.

Oil and natural gas are the state's most important natural resources. More than 80 percent of the taxes collected by the state come from the oil and gas industry. Most of Alaska's known oil deposits are in the far north. The Trans-Alaska Pipeline, which extends north-south for 800 miles, transports most of the oil produced in the state to Valdez, in southern Alaska.

Much of Alaska's oil is found beneath the ocean and can be accessed through offshore drilling.

Plants

From forest to marsh, Alaska has a variety of plant life. Among Alaska's plant life are bushes that produce juicy berries, including the lowbush cranberry, strawberries, blueberries, and cloudberries. Pine forests are found in many of Alaska's highlands and along the coast. Other trees that are common in Alaska are spruce, cottonwood, Alaska birch, and larch. Tongass National Forest and Chugach National Forest are the largest national forests in the United States.

Alaska's small human population and untouched wilderness areas keep the state's environment pure and healthy. Plants that have been in Alaska for thousands of years continue to exist. However, as more people have sought to make use of the many resources found in the state, some of these plants have become **threatened**.

MONKSHOOD

Monkshood is beautiful to look at, but all parts of the plant are poisonous if ingested.

LINGONBERRIES, OR LOWBUSH CRANBERRIES

The lingonberry, or lowbush cranberry, is the most common berry growing in Alaska.

BOREAL, OR NORTHERN, FOREST

Boreal forests are found in Alaska's interior. They are the product of extreme temperatures and slow, short growing periods.

BIRCH TREES

Three varieties of birch trees grow in Alaska. One kind, Kenai canoe birch, has been used by Alaska Natives to make canoes.

In the summertime, wildflowers are plentiful in Alaska's natural regions.

A poisonous berry found in Alaska is the baneberry. Baneberries may be either red or white.

Berries are one of the traditional foods of the Inuit people.

Reindeer lichen grow in the tundra of Alaska and serve as food for caribou, moose, reindeer, and other animals living there. Reindeer lichen are actually a combination of two different kinds of living things, an alga and a fungus.

Animals

Alaska is home to a wide variety of animals in the sky, on land, and in water. There are about 400 different bird species in Alaska. The eagle is the largest bird found in the state. Other common birds include owls, hawks, and falcons. The Arctic tern, found in Alaska during the summer, spends the winter in Antarctica, some 10,000 miles away.

Bears are common in Alaska. Brown bears (also known as grizzly bears), black bears, and polar bears all make their home in the state. Also found in Alaska are beavers, reindeer, wolverines, wolves, deer, elks, bison, foxes, moose, mountain sheep, mountain goats, and lynx.

Alaska's waters are home to many fish and marine mammals. More than a dozen different species of whales can be seen off Alaska's coast. They include the bowhead whale, the humpback whale, the killer whale, and the narwhal. Other sea animals include otters, walruses, and seals.

SOCKEYE SALMON

Every spring, millions of salmon return to Alaska to **spawn**. Adult salmon may swim as far as 2,000 miles.

AMERICAN BALD EAGLE

The bald eagle was officially adopted as the U.S. national emblem on June 20, 1782. Many bald eagles make their home in Alaska.

POLAR BEAR

The polar bear is now listed as a threatened species, because of melting ice in the northern sea and oceans.

HUMPBACK WHALE

Humpback whales frequent the seas around Alaska in the spring, summer, and autumn. In the winter they travel to warmer waters around Mexico or Hawai'i.

Tourism

Tourism is a highly profitable industry in Alaska that has grown in the past several decades. Most visitors come from elsewhere in the United States. Because of Alaska's cold winters and mild summers, most tourists come to the state during summer.

Cruise ships sail along Alaska's coast and bring passengers to the state. Many of the cruises begin in Canada or Seattle, Washington, and sail along the Inside Passage, a waterway between Alaska's southeastern coast and offshore islands. A favorite part of these trips is Glacier Bay, where visitors admire the beautiful ice forms.

Some of the most popular tourist destinations in Alaska are Portage Glacier, Mount McKinley, Skagway's historical gold rush district, and the Anchorage Museum of History and Art. The Ketchikan Totems and Sitka's Russian church and dancers also draw large numbers of tourists.

CRUISING THE INSIDE PASSAGE

Seeing Alaska from the deck of a cruise ship is a popular vacation trip. Some cruises offer land tours before or after the cruise.

RUSSIAN CHURCHES

St. Nicholas Russian Orthodox Church in Juneau is the oldest church in Alaska. It was consecrated in 1894.

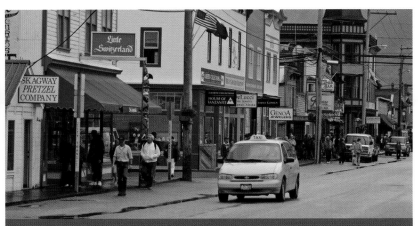

KLONDIKE GOLD RUSH NATIONAL HISTORIC PARK

The city of Skagway is located within the boundaries of Klondike Gold Rush National Historic Park. It is one of only two U.S. cities within a National Park Service site.

DENALI NATIONAL PARK

Denali National Park is one of the most popular tourist destinations in Alaska. It attracts more than 425,000 visitors a year.

Alaska welcomes about 1.6 million visitors each year. About 60 percent travel to the state by cruise ship, and many others come by plane.

More than 30,000 Alaskans work in the tourism industry during the peak season. Because the tourist industry is seasonal, unemployment in Alaska varies greatly over the course of a year.

Ecotourism is responsible travel to natural areas that preserves the environment and improves the well-being of local people. Alaska is a prime year-round destination for ecotourists. Guided ecotours can be arranged to most of the national parks, forests, wildlife refuges, and preserves in Alaska. Adventure Green Alaska certifies businesses that meet established standards for sustainability.

Industry

Alaska's first major industry was the fur trade. Russian explorers took furs back to Russia to sell. Though fur trapping still exists in Alaska, it now occurs on a much smaller scale.

The gold industry brought the next big flow of money into the state. Like the fur trade, gold mining continues in Alaska but on a much smaller scale.

Industries in Alaska
Value of Goods and Services in Millions of Dollars

The pie chart below shows how important different industries are to Alaska. What is the largest industry in the state? In which categories do you think tourism plays a role?

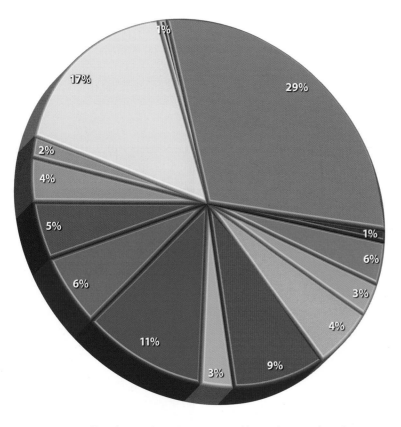

LEGEND

Agriculture, Forestry, and Fishing	$381
Mining	$14,251
Utilities	$584
Construction	$1,926
Manufacturing	$1,543
Wholesale and Retail Trade	$2,936
Transportation	$4,476
Media and Entertainment	$1,358
Finance, Insurance, and Real Estate	$5,429
Professional and Technical Services	$2,810
* Education	$130
Health Care	$2,376
Hotels and Restaurants	$1,180
Other Services	$812
Government	$8,358
TOTAL	**$48,550**

*Less than 1%. Percentages may not add to 100 because of rounding.

The oil and natural gas industry became important in Alaska in the 1970s. A large oil field was discovered near Prudhoe Bay in 1968. Geologists estimated that it was twice as large as any other oil field in North America at the time. Several oil companies joined together to build the Trans-Alaska Pipeline, which was then the largest privately funded construction project in history. The pipeline, which cost $8 billion to build, is operated by the Alyeska Pipeline Service Company. It is one of the top tourist attractions in the state.

Today more Alaskans work in the service sector than in any other part of the economy. Tourism and the government are leading service employers. Timber and fishing are other major industries in the state.

The second-largest oil spill in U.S. history occurred off the Alaska coast. On March 24, 1989, a tanker called the Exxon Valdez *spilled 11 million gallons of oil into Prince William Sound. The spill stretched for more than 450 miles.*

I DIDN'T KNOW THAT!

About 70,000 workers were involved in building the Trans-Alaska Pipeline. The pipeline, which has a diameter of 48 inches, runs from Prudhoe Bay to the port of Valdez.

The 800-mile Trans-Alaska Pipeline runs underground for about half its length. The other half of the pipeline is aboveground, held up by supports.

Tongass and Chugach national forests contain much of Alaska's timber resources.

Goods and Services

F ew goods and services can be found outside the major population centers in Alaska. The best place for people to find what they need is in Anchorage. Most goods found in Anchorage have been flown into the city from elsewhere in the United States. The state's largest airport also is in Anchorage. It is one of the leading handlers of **cargo** in the United States. Some Alaskans are dependent on air travel for the distribution of goods because not all areas have roads or railroads. In fact, Alaska has more registered pilots **per capita** than any other state.

The four major sectors driving Anchorage's local economy are oil and gas, the military, transportation, and tourism. Although Anchorage is not the center of oil and gas production, it is the administrative center for the industry in Alaska.

Because so many goods and materials have to be brought into the state, Alaska has a high cost of living. Providing services and medical care to remote areas in Alaska is expensive. Also, the cost of goods is high because there is little or no competition. In some smaller towns food may cost up to double what it costs in other places in the United States. Although the cost of living in Alaska is high, so are most of the salaries people earn. By charging more for their services, Alaskans can offset the high cost of living.

Much of Alaska's employment is seasonal. During summer the unemployment rate is much lower than it is in winter.

According to some studies, three of the top 10 most expensive U.S. cities to live in are found in Alaska. These cities are Anchorage, Fairbanks, and Juneau.

The government is a large employer in Alaska. Almost one of every five workers in Alaska works for the federal, state, or local governments.

The University of Alaska has a main campus in Fairbanks, as well as campuses in Anchorage and Juneau. First known as the Alaska Agricultural College and School of Mines, the Fairbanks campus opened its doors in 1922.

Both residents and tourists fish the waters of Alaska's lakes and seas. Many fishers enjoy the Togiak River off Bristol Bay, where hundreds of thousands of salmon return to spawn every year.

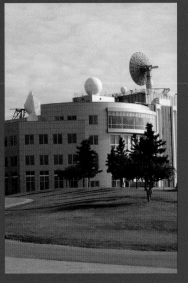

Alaska Natives

Many scientists believe that people have been living in Alaska for 15,000 years or more. The first people to live in North America may have walked from eastern Russia to Alaska over a land bridge that connected the two areas during the last Ice Age, when sea levels were lower than they are today. These people were the **ancestors** of today's American Indians.

Other Alaska Natives who are not Indians may have come to Alaska from eastern Asia by boat or by walking over frozen seas. These groups include the Inuit (or Eskimo) and the Aleut peoples.

The peoples who first settled the Alaska region brought with them their own beliefs about their origins. These beliefs explain how the land was created and how they came to live on it.

Some Eskimo children live on islands that are reachable only by air and that have been inhabited for thousands of years.

American Indian groups living in Alaska today include a number of peoples in central and northern Alaska who speak related Athabascan languages. American Indian groups in Alaska also include the Northwest Coast peoples of southeastern Alaska, such as the Tlingit, Haida, and Tsimshian peoples.

The cultures of all of Alaska's native peoples are still rich and alive. While many Alaska Natives live modern lives, some still rely for food on traditional methods of hunting and fishing. Many Alaska Natives keep their traditions alive, telling the stories, singing the songs, and dancing the dances that have come down to them from their ancestors.

The Inuit people keep their traditions alive by hunting whales in small sealskin-made boats called umiaks. Inuit women sew sealskins together, to be stretched over the frame of the boat.

I DIDN'T KNOW THAT!

The Aleutian Islands are named after the Aleut people.

The Bering Land Bridge National Preserve is located near the site of the original land bridge between Russia and Alaska. Native Inupiat people still live on the land preserve, following a lifestyle that has existed for thousands of years.

The totem poles found in Alaska are made by the Northwest Coast Indians. These peoples also still practice the potlatch, which is the ceremonial distribution of property and gifts.

A large expedition arrived by boat in the late 1700s at Sitka, the capital of Russian Alaska, under the command of Aleksandr Baranov, the first Russian governor of Alaska.

Explorers

I n the 1720s, Tsar Peter the Great of Russia sent Vitus Bering to explore the North Pacific Ocean. His goal was to find a northeastern sea route to China around Siberia. Because of bad weather, Bering was unable to see the North American coast on this trip. In 1741, during the reign of Empress Anna, he made a second voyage, and this time he came upon what is now Alaska. Bering died during the return journey. The Russian island on which he is buried is now named Bering Island in his honor. His crew members brought back high-quality sea otter furs from Alaska. This led to other Russian expeditions, and soon a number of camps had been set up from which Russians trapped sea otters and other fur-bearing animals or traded with the native peoples for furs.

In 1784, the first permanent European settlement in what is now Alaska was built on Kodiak Island. From there Aleksandr Baranov controlled the trapping and trading posts on the mainland. Although Russians controlled Alaska during the late 1700s, explorers from other countries also came to the area, including Captain James Cook and George Vancouver of Great Britain and Juan Perez of Spain.

Timeline of Settlement

Early Exploration

1741 Vitus Bering, a Dane exploring for Russia, lands near Mount St. Elias.

1742 Bering crew members bring furs back to Russia.

Russian Settlement

1784 Grigory Shelekhov establishes the first European settlement near present-day Kodiak.

1806 The Russian-American Company, which is allowed by the Russian government to control the fur trade in Alaska, moves its headquarters to Sitka.

1824 Russia signs treaties with the United States and Great Britain, establishing trade boundaries and commercial regulations in Alaska.

United States Possession

1867 After negotiations led by Secretary of State William Seward, the United States purchases Alaska from Russia for $7.2 million.

1878 Salmon canneries are built in Alaska, starting what was to become the largest salmon industry in the world.

1897–1900 The Klondike Gold Rush brings thousands of settlers to Alaska.

United States Territory

1912 Alaska becomes a U.S. territory.

1942 The Japanese invade the Aleutian Islands during World War II.

1942–1945 The Japanese invasion prompts construction of airfields and the Alaska Highway, which contribute to settlement after the war.

Statehood and After

1959 Alaska becomes the 49th state.

1968 The largest oil field in North America is discovered near Prudhoe Bay.

Early Settlers

I n the mid-1800s, Russia lost interest in Alaska because it was not seeing enough of a profit from the fur trade. Russia offered to sell the land to the United States. U.S. Secretary of State William Seward negotiated a treaty with Russia for the purchase. The treaty, signed in 1867, paid the Russian government $7.2 million for the region. This was less than two cents an acre.

Map of Settlements and Resources in Early Alaska

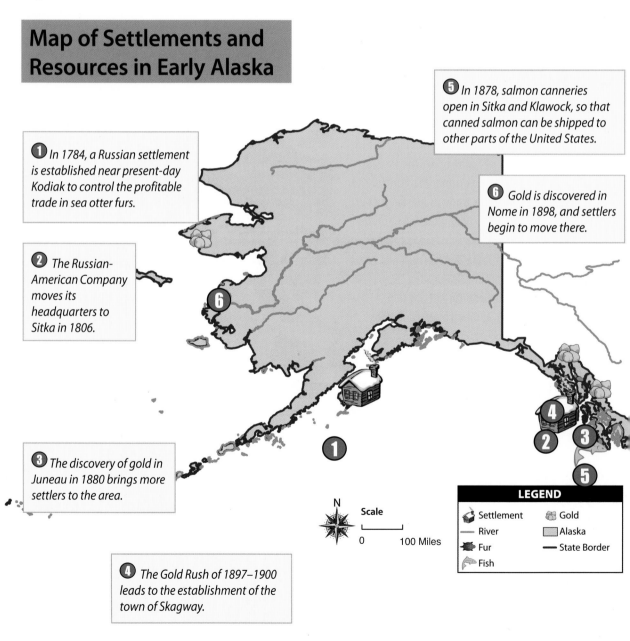

5 In 1878, salmon canneries open in Sitka and Klawock, so that canned salmon can be shipped to other parts of the United States.

1 In 1784, a Russian settlement is established near present-day Kodiak to control the profitable trade in sea otter furs.

6 Gold is discovered in Nome in 1898, and settlers begin to move there.

2 The Russian-American Company moves its headquarters to Sitka in 1806.

3 The discovery of gold in Juneau in 1880 brings more settlers to the area.

4 The Gold Rush of 1897–1900 leads to the establishment of the town of Skagway.

N

Scale

0   100 Miles

LEGEND

Settlement	Gold
River	Alaska
Fur	State Border
Fish	

Newspapers in the United States strongly criticized Seward for the purchase. Many believed Alaska had little to offer the United States. They referred to the deal as "Seward's Folly" and to Alaska as "Seward's Icebox." Despite the objections, the U.S. Senate approved the treaty. Seward's critics quickly forgave him when gold was discovered in the region in the 1870s and 1880s.

The discovery of gold encouraged many settlers to come to Alaska in search of fortune. Large gold deposits were found near Nome, Juneau, and Fairbanks. Many of the early settlers were not prepared for Alaska's cold climate. Those who came unprepared faced starvation and exposure to freezing temperatures. Settlers came so quickly that there were few government laws to control the masses. Alaska became known as the Wild North.

Gold discoveries were made in the neighboring Yukon Territory as well. Traffic through Alaska increased as prospectors made their way to Canada. Settlements grew into communities with churches, newspapers, and other services. In 1906, Juneau replaced Sitka as Alaska's capital. In the same year Alaska adopted a code of laws and a court system.

The discovery of gold brought many settlers to Alaska. In the Klondike gold fields, miners had to carry all of their equipment on their backs, trudging over the Chilkoot Pass by foot.

Notable People

Many notable Alaskans have contributed to the development of their state and their country. These include Alaska Natives who helped win equality for their people. They also include a man who helped to make Alaska a state and a teenager who created the Alaskan flag. In addition, several writers have communicated the beauty and wonder of Alaska to the world as a whole.

LEONHARD SEPPALA
(1877–1967)

Leonhard Seppala is one of the greatest sled-dog racers Alaska has ever known. He was born in Norway and came to Alaska as a young man, attracted by the Gold Rush. In 1914, he began to win sled dog races and became a legend in his own time. He is most known for rushing diphtheria medicine to Nome, Alaska, in 1925, when the city faced a deadly outbreak of the disease.

ERNEST GRUENING
(1887–1974)

When Alaska was still a territory, Ernest Gruening served as both the governor and a senator, although he could not yet vote in the Senate. He led the drive for Alaska's statehood and then served as senator from Alaska from 1959 to 1969.

CARL BEN EIELSON (1897–1929)

Carl Ben Eielson trained to be a pilot during World War I. In 1925, he was the first person to fly over the polar ice cap, from Alaska to Greenland. Eielson died in a plane crash in 1929, while trying to rescue passengers aboard a ship caught in the ice off the Siberian coast.

ELIZABETH PERATROVICH (1911–1958)

A Tlingit Indian, Elizabeth Peratrovich was no stranger to discrimination in Alaska. In 1945, Peratrovich provided testimony to the Alaska Senate that led to the passage of an antidiscrimination law. This law required equal treatment for all citizens in public accommodations.

JOHN BEN "BENNY" BENSON (1913–1972)

In 1927, 13-year-old Benny Benson's design for a flag for Alaska was chosen in a contest. When Alaska became a state, the drafters of the Alaska constitution required that Benson's design become the official flag of the state of Alaska. Benson worked as a carpenter and mechanic for Kodiak Airways until his death in 1972.

I DIDN'T KNOW THAT!

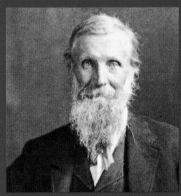

John Muir (1838–1914) is widely regarded as the father of the national parks movement in the United States. He made seven trips to Alaska and wrote several books about these journeys. He once wrote, "To the lover of pure wildness Alaska is one of the most wonderful countries in the world."

Jean Craighead George (1919–), an author, traveled to Alaska in the late 1960s to learn about wolf behavior. Based on meetings with Inuit people there, George wrote a novel about a girl who is lost on the tundra and who communicates with wolves. *Julie of the Wolves* won the Newbery Award in 1973.

Population

A lthough Alaska's population is small, it has steadily increased over the past several decades. In 1980, Alaska's population was just over 400,000. By 2000 the state had more than 625,000 residents, an increase of more than 50 percent in those 20 years. By 2010, the state had more than 710,000 residents. About 286,000 people live in the state's largest city, Anchorage. Fairbanks is home to about 35,000 people, and Juneau, about 31,000. Wasilla is the only other city in the state to have more than 10,000 residents, and numerous cities have fewer than 150 residents.

Alaska Population 1950-2010

Alaska's population has been growing in every decade since 1950. What are some of the reasons that many people have chosen to move to Alaska in recent decades?

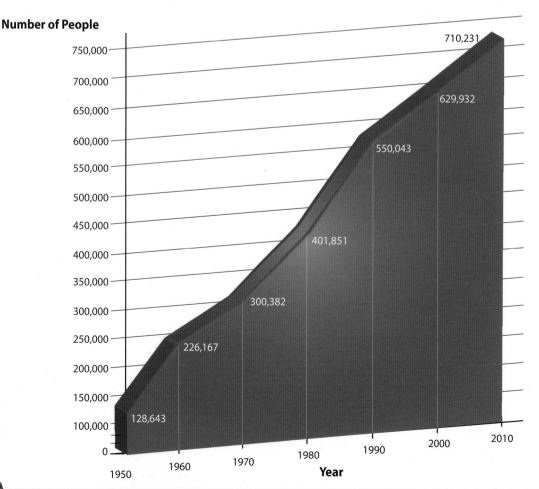

Number of People

Alaska Native children used to have to travel far from home to attend school. Now many attend small schools within their communities.

Many of today's Alaskans are descendants of early Russian settlers or of Americans and Canadians who came in search of gold in the late 1800s. Native peoples account for about 15 percent of Alaska's population. Although some Alaska Natives live in cities, most live in smaller towns and villages. The state's population also includes small numbers of Hispanics, African Americans, and Asian Americans. Most of these people live in cities.

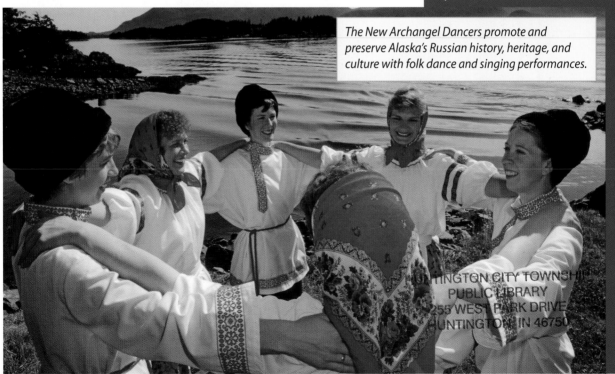

The New Archangel Dancers promote and preserve Alaska's Russian history, heritage, and culture with folk dance and singing performances.

Politics and Government

L ike each state in the Union, Alaska is governed on local, state, and federal levels. The state has a governor and a lieutenant governor, both of whom are elected to four-year terms. The governor appoints the head of each of the 14 state departments. The state legislature has two chambers, the Senate and the House of Representatives. Forty representatives are elected to the House every two years. Twenty senators are elected every four years. Local government is not divided into counties as in other states. Instead, the state is divided into cities and **boroughs**.

The Alaska State Capitol Building in Juneau was completed in 1931, when Alaska was a territory.

On January 3, 1959, Alaska became the 49th state to join the Union. The only state admitted to the Union after Alaska was Hawaii. Alaska is represented in Washington, D.C., by two members of the U.S. Senate and one member of the U.S. House of Representatives.

In 1971 the U.S. Congress approved the Claims Settlement Act. This act granted 44 million acres of land and more than $950 million to Alaska's native peoples.

Sarah Palin, former governor of Alaska, ran for vice president of the United States in 2008 as a Republican.

Alaska's state song is called "Alaska's Flag."

Here is an excerpt from the song:

*Eight stars of gold on a field
  of blue,
Alaska's flag, may it mean
  to you,
The blue of the sea, the
  evening sky,
The mountain lakes and
  the flowers nearby,*

*The gold of the early
  sourdough's dreams,
The precious gold of the
  hills and streams,
The brilliant stars in the
  northern sky,
The "Bear," the "Dipper,"
  and shining high,*

*The great North Star with
  its steady light,
O'er land and sea a
  beacon bright,
Alaska's flag to Alaskans dear,
The simple flag of a last
  frontier.*

Cultural Groups

Alaska Natives make up the largest minority group in Alaska. Long before Russians or other explorers first traveled to the region, native peoples, including the Inuit, Aleuts, and American Indian groups, had their own rich cultures. They had their own belief systems, ceremonies, and arts and crafts. They used the resources available to them for practical and ceremonial purposes. For example, they carved ivory from walrus tusks to make harpoon heads and knife handles. They also carved dolls and sculptures from ivory. Jade and soapstone were also used in carvings. Many of the ancient arts and crafts traditions of Alaska Natives continue today.

Many Alaska Natives now live in towns and cities and work in mines or oil fields. They continue to gather for traditional community celebrations, which often center around the seasons.

The Northwest Coast Indians who live in the southeastern part of the state continue to build totem poles. Totem poles are carved from huge cedar trees. They record the history, culture, and life events of the people who carve them. Totem poles include symbols for ancestors or **clans**. They are painted with vegetable or mineral dyes.

Often, when people think of living in Alaska, igloos come to mind. Very few people use igloos anymore. However, igloos are still used by Inuit hunters out on the frozen ocean or tundra. They are built as temporary shelters for the period of the hunt.

Totem poles still play an important role in the lives of some Alaskan people.

I DIDN'T KNOW THAT!

Igloo means "snowhouse."

Animals important to the Northwest Coast peoples are shown on their totem poles. These animals include eagles, whales, wolves, bears, ravens, beavers, and frogs.

The Haida people of Alaska used copper as a sign of wealth. Copper plaques were etched and shaped into shields. "Coppers" were given names and histories, and they were considered very powerful.

Some traditional foods of Alaska Natives are meat, fish, and berries.

Beadwork is a common craft among Indian women.

The Aleuts are known for their excellent basket weaving skills.

The expression "low man on the totem pole" is misleading. The bottom 10 feet of a totem pole are usually carved by a master carver, while **apprentices** complete the rest. The characters at the bottom of the totem pole are usually the most significant.

Arts and Entertainment

Although the northern lights are not an art form, they could be. Also called the aurora borealis, these dancing lights provide one of the best forms of entertainment in the state. Northern lights are naturally occurring colored lights in the upper atmosphere. They are most visible near Earth's magnetic poles. Fairbanks is considered one of the best places in the world to see the northern lights.

Anchorage is an excellent place to be immersed in Alaskan culture. The city boasts art galleries, museums, theaters, a symphony orchestra, and an opera house. The Anchorage Museum of History and Art houses a gallery showing works of art from Alaska and around the world. The museum also displays artifacts from several Alaskan cultures.

The northern lights are a spectacular display in Alaska's skies.

The Heritage Library and Museum in Anchorage features artwork by Alaska Natives and other Alaskans, including tools, paintings, costumes, and beadwork. Anchorage has the largest museums, but many other fine museums can be found across the state.

Alaska hosts numerous festivals, fairs, and celebrations throughout the year. Many festivals occur during the summer months, when the sun shines almost around the clock. Most towns have activities to celebrate the **summer solstice**.

The pop singer Jewel grew up on an 800-acre homestead in Homer, Alaska. Her first hit single, "Who Will Save Your Soul," earned her an MTV Video Music Awards nomination for Best Female Video in 1996.

Sports

One of the most popular sports in Alaska is dog mushing, or dogsled racing. In fact, it was adopted as Alaska's official state sport in 1972. Hundreds of races ranging from local matches to world championships are held every year. There are different kinds of races, from sprint mushing to long-distance racing. Winners of sprint races are determined by speed, often over distances of 12 to 15 miles. Long-distance races can take many days, even weeks, as the racers travel great distances.

The Iditarod Trail Sled Dog Race is one of the oldest races run in Alaska. First held as a 56-mile race in 1967, the Iditarod was made into a much longer 1,100-mile race in 1973. The race starts in Anchorage and goes up and across the state, ending in Nome. Today winners often take about nine days to finish the course.

All-Star forward Carlos Boozer of the National Basketball Association's Chicago Bulls grew up in Juneau.

For four days in July, native peoples from Alaska, the Pacific Northwest, and Canada gather in Fairbanks for the World Eskimo-Indian Olympics. Traditional Alaskan competitions are held, including ear-pulling, a four-man carry, knuckle hopping, and **high kicking**. The World Eskimo-Indian Olympics begin with a race called the Race of the Torch. The race winner lights the Olympic torch that year.

For nature lovers, kayaking, cross-country skiing, and white-water rafting are great ways to see the state.

Dog mushing is a popular pastime in Alaska.

National Averages Comparison

T he United States is a federal republic, consisting of fifty states and the District of Columbia. Alaska and Hawai'i are the only non-contiguous, or non-touching, states in the nation. Today, the United States of America is the third-largest country in the world in population. The United States Census Bureau takes a census, or count of all the people, every ten years. It also regularly collects other kinds of data about the population and the economy. How does Alaska compare to the national average?

Comparison Chart

United States 2010 Census Data *	USA	Alaska
Admission to Union	NA	January 3, 1959
Land Area (in square miles)	3,537,438.44	571,951.26
Population Total	308,745,538	710,231
Population Density (people per square mile)	87.28	1.24
Population Percentage Change (April 1, 2000, to April 1, 2010)	9.7%	13.3%
White Persons (percent)	72.4%	66.7%
Black Persons (percent)	12.6%	3.3%
American Indian and Alaska Native Persons (percent)	0.9%	14.8%
Asian Persons (percent)	4.8%	5.4%
Native Hawaiian and Other Pacific Islander Persons (percent)	0.2%	1.0%
Some Other Race (percent)	6.2%	1.6%
Persons Reporting Two or More Races (percent)	2.9%	7.3%
Persons of Hispanic or Latino Origin (percent)	16.3%	5.5%
Not of Hispanic or Latino Origin (percent)	83.7%	94.5%
Median Household Income	$52,029	$67,332
Percentage of People Age 25 or Over Who Have Graduated from High School	80.4%	88.3%

*All figures are based on the 2010 United States Census, with the exception of the last two items. Percentages may not add to 100 because of rounding.

How to Improve My Community

Strong communities make strong states. Think about what features are important in your community. What do you value? Education? Health? Forests? Safety? Beautiful spaces? Government works to help citizens create ideal living conditions that are fair to all by providing services in communities. Consider what changes you could make in your community. How would they improve your state as a whole? Using this concept web as a guide, write a report that outlines the features you think are most important in your community and what improvements could be made. A strong state needs strong communities.

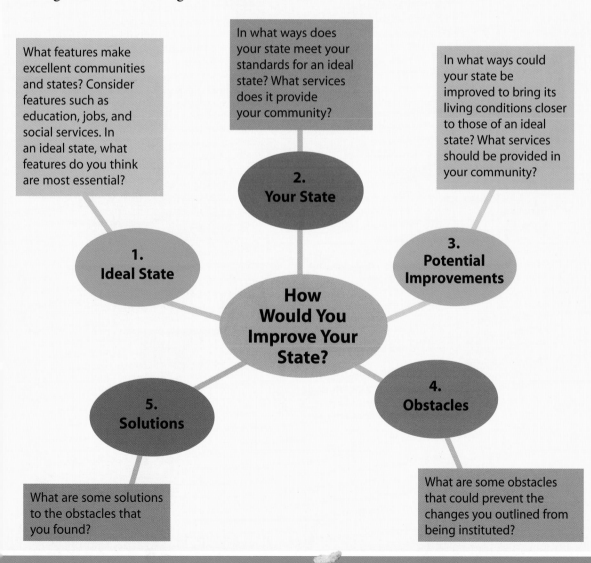

What features make excellent communities and states? Consider features such as education, jobs, and social services. In an ideal state, what features do you think are most essential?

In what ways does your state meet your standards for an ideal state? What services does it provide your community?

In what ways could your state be improved to bring its living conditions closer to those of an ideal state? What services should be provided in your community?

2. Your State

1. Ideal State

3. Potential Improvements

How Would You Improve Your State?

5. Solutions

4. Obstacles

What are some solutions to the obstacles that you found?

What are some obstacles that could prevent the changes you outlined from being instituted?

Exercise Your Mind!

Think about these questions and then use your research skills to find the answers and learn more fascinating facts about Alaska. A teacher, librarian, or parent may be able to help you locate the best sources to use in your research.

1 Mount McKinley is the highest peak in North America. How high is it?

2 How many of the 20 highest mountain peaks in the United States are in Alaska?

3 By what other names has Mount McKinley been known?

4 How was the Valley of Ten Thousand Smokes created?

5 How many lakes does Alaska have?

6 Alaska is host to the largest gathering of bald eagles in the world. Where does this take place?

7 Is it possible to experience an earthquake in Alaska?

8 What is the only U.S. capital that cannot be reached by road?

Words to Know

ancestors: ancient relatives

apprentices: people who learn by working under the guidance of a skilled master

boroughs: units of local government similar to counties in other states

cargo: goods transported by ships, trucks, and airplanes

clans: groups of families

exports: shipments to other countries

glaciers: large, slow-moving sheets of ice

high kicking: an Inuit sporting activity in which competitors jump up and kick a hanging object

per capita: in relation to the size of a population

pontoons: floating devices attached to seaplanes

prospectors: individuals who search for gold

spawn: to give birth

summer solstice: the beginning of summer in the Northern Hemisphere

threatened: referring to a type of plant or animal that is likely to become endangered, or at risk of disappearing from Earth

tundra: large, treeless plains in the Arctic with a top layer that remains frozen throughout the year

Index

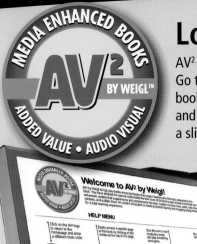

Log on to www.av2books.com

AV² by Weigl brings you media enhanced books that support active learning. Go to www.av2books.com, and enter the special code found on page 2 of this book. You will gain access to enriched and enhanced content that supplements and complements this book. Content includes video, audio, web links, quizzes, a slide show, and activities.

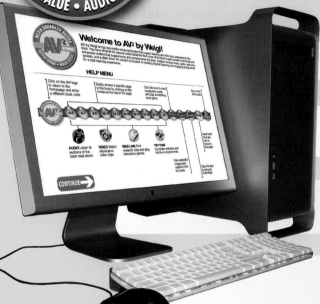

Audio
Listen to sections of the book read aloud.

Video
Watch informative video clips.

Embedded Weblinks
Gain additional information for research.

Try This!
Complete activities and hands-on experiments.

WHAT'S ONLINE?

Try This!	**Embedded Weblinks**	**Video**	**EXTRA FEATURES**
Test your knowledge of the state in a mapping activity.	Discover more attractions in Alaska.	Watch a video introduction to Alaska.	**Audio** Listen to sections of the book read aloud.
Find out more about precipitation in your city.	Learn more about the history of the state.	Watch a video about the features of the state.	
Plan what attractions you would like to visit in the state.	Learn the full lyrics of the state song.		**Key Words** Study vocabulary, and complete a matching word activity.
Learn more about the early natural resources of the state.			
Write a biography about a notable resident of Alaska.			**Slide Show** View images and captio and prepare a presenta
Complete an educational census activity.			**Quizzes** Test your knowledge.

AV² was built to bridge the gap between print and digital. We encourage you to tell us what you like and what you want to see in the future.

Sign up to be an AV² Ambassador at www.av2books.com/ambassador.